WHEN YOUR WAY ISN'T WORKING

Finding Purpose and Contentment through Deep Connection with Jesus

BIBLE STUDY GUIDE | FIVE SESSIONS

KYLE IDLEMAN

WITH REBECCA ENGLISH LAWSON

Chapters 11 & 12

HarperChristian
Resources

When Your Way Isn't Working Bible Study Guide
© 2023 Kyle Idleman

Requests for information should be addressed to:
HarperChristian Resources, 3900 Sparks Dr. SE, Grand Rapids, Michigan 49546

ISBN: 978-0-310-14052-8 (softcover)
ISBN: 978-0-310-14053-5 (e-book)

HarperChristian Resources titles may be purchased in bulk for church, business, fundraising, or ministry use. For information, please e-mail ResourceSpecialist@ChurchSource.com.

Published in association with the literary agency of The Gates Group, 1403 Walnut Lane, Louisville, KY 40223.

First printing April 2023 / Printed in the United States of America

23 24 25 26 27 LBC 5 4 3 2 1

CONTENTS

SESSION 4: THE PURPOSE OF PRUNING

SESSION 5: GRAFTED AND GROWING

A NOTE FROM

KYLE IDLEMAN

Sometimes, we're the last to notice it when our way isn't working.

For far too long, my way wasn't working. My approach to handling that reality was to try to make things work. Not to brag, but I'm really good at not asking people for help. Like super good at it. It's much more appealing for me to be a rescuer than the person getting rescued. No one watches *Spiderman* and dreams about being the person hanging from the balcony hoping to be saved. So it took awhile, but I finally realized that I needed a different way.

I found it in the words of Jesus to his closest followers in John 15. Jesus was down to his final moments with his disciples. They didn't realize this was the end of their time with him on earth . . . but he did. Jesus also knew that eleven of his twelve disciples were going to take the gospel to the ends of the earth. He knew the challenges that they would face in that calling. And he knew that if the disciples tried to do things their way, it just wouldn't work.

Listen to what Jesus says to them in that chapter: "I am the vine; you are the branches. If you remain in me and I in you, you will bear much fruit; apart from me you can do nothing" (John 15:5). That phrase, "you can do nothing," captures the exasperation of our way not working. We put in the work, but we don't see the results.

When nothing we're doing seems to be working, we need to understand this metaphor that Jesus gave his disciples. It all comes down to one word: *connection*. Jesus is the vine, and we are the branches. As long as we, the branches, stay connected to him, the vine, we will bear much fruit. But apart from Jesus, nothing will really work the way it should.

Jesus says to us, "No matter what happens, no matter how discouraged you are, no matter how disappointed you are, no matter how frustrating a situation might be, no matter how tired you feel, no matter what kind of trouble you experience, the one thing you must never forget is stay connected." As branches, our *only* job is to stay connected to Jesus. Maybe that seems too passive . . . too simple. But the personal practices you need to live a life deeply connected to the Lord don't just happen. They require intentionality.

If you have found that your way just isn't working, it's time to check your connection to the vine. If you are discouraged, frustrated, anxious, and worn out, it's time to stop trying to be the vine and instead be the branch. When you begin to humbly depend on the vine, you will begin to bear much fruit—and you will bring God glory.

— KYLE IDLEMAN

HOW TO USE THIS GUIDE

We all want to be part of something bigger than ourselves—to lead lives of connection, productivity, and purpose. Often, however, in our efforts to find meaning, we connect with the wrong things, and what we thought would produce a harvest ultimately leaves us tired, empty, and dry. We find that our way doesn't work.

In this study, we will draw on Jesus' words to his disciples in John 15 and explore what those words teach us about connection and purpose. We will examine how connection begins with Jesus—and how when our way isn't working, it's because there is a break somewhere in the connection with him. When we stay close to Jesus, his life will flow into us, and the result will be fruitfulness beyond anything we could have produced on our own.

Before you begin this study, keep in mind that there are a few ways you can go through this material. You can experience the study with others in a small group (such as a Bible study, Sunday school class, or home group), or you may choose to go through the content on your own. Either way, the videos for each session are available for you to view at any time by following the instructions provided on the inside cover of this study guide.

GROUP STUDY

Each of the sessions in this study guide are divided into two parts: (1) a group study section and (2) a personal study section. The group study section provides a basic framework on how to open your time together, get the most out of the video content, and discuss the key ideas together that were presented in the teaching. Each session includes the following:

- **Welcome:** A short note about the topic of the session for you to read on your own before you meet as a group.
- **Connect:** A few icebreaker questions to get you and your group members thinking about the topic and interacting with each other.

- **Watch:** An outline of the key points covered in each video teaching along with space for you to take notes as you watch each session.
- **Discuss:** Questions to help you and your group reflect on the teaching material presented and apply it to your lives.
- **Respond:** A short personal exercise to help reinforce the key ideas.
- **Pray:** A place for you to record prayer requests and praises for the week.

If you are doing this study in a group, make sure you have your own copy of the study guide so you can write down your thoughts, responses, and reflections—and so you will have access to the videos via streaming. You will also want to have a copy of the *When Your Way Isn't Working* book, as reading it alongside the curriculum will provide you with deeper insights. (See the notes at the beginning of each group session and personal study section on which chapters of the book you should read before the next group session.)

Finally, keep these points in mind:

- **Facilitation:** If you are doing this study in a group, you will want to appoint someone to serve as a facilitator. This person will be responsible for starting the video and keeping track of time during discussions and activities. If *you* have been chosen for this role, there are some resources in the back of this guide that can help you lead your group through the study.

- **Faithfulness:** Your group is a place where tremendous growth can happen as you reflect on the Bible, ask questions, and learn what God is doing in other people's lives. For this reason, be fully committed and attend each session so you can build trust and rapport with the other members.

- **Friendship:** The goal of any small group is to serve as a place where people can share, learn about God, and build friendships. So make your group a "safe place." Be honest about your thoughts and feelings, but also listen carefully to everyone else's thoughts, feelings, and opinions. Keep anything personal that your group members share in confidence so that you can create a community where people can heal, be challenged, and grow spiritually.

If you are going through this study on your own, read the opening Welcome section and reflect on the questions in the Connect section. Watch the video and use the prompts that have been provided to take notes. Finally, personalize the questions and exercises in the Discuss and Respond sections. Close by recording any requests you want to pray about during the week.

PERSONAL STUDY

The personal study is for you to work through on your own during the week. Each exercise is designed to help you explore the key ideas you uncovered during your group time and delve into passages of Scripture that will help you apply those principles to your life. Go at your own pace, doing a little each day—or tackle the material all at once. Remember to spend a few moments in silence to listen to whatever the Holy Spirit might be saying to you.

Each section contains three personal studies that open with a brief devotion for you to read, a few passages for you to look up, and several reflection questions to help you apply the truths of God's Word to your life. Following this, there is a Connect & Discuss page with several questions for you to answer with a friend, either over a phone call or a cup of coffee. Finally, the Catch Up & Read Ahead page will give you a chance to finish any uncompleted personal studies and read the upcoming chapters in *When Your Way Isn't Working*.

Note that if you are doing this study as part of a group, and are unable to finish (or even start) these personal studies for the week, you should still attend the group time. Be assured that you are wanted and welcome even if you don't have your "homework" done. The group studies and personal studies are intended to help you hear what God wants you to hear and how to apply what he is saying to your life. So . . . as you go through this study, be listening for him to speak to you as you learn about what it means to remain connected to Jesus.

WEEK 1

BEFORE GROUP MEETING	Read chapters 1–3 in *When Your Way Isn't Working* Read the Welcome section (page 3)
GROUP MEETING	Discuss the Connect questions Watch the video teaching for session 1 Discuss the questions that follow as a group Do the closing exercise and pray (pages 3–8)
STUDY 1	Complete the personal study (pages 10–12)
STUDY 2	Complete the personal study (pages 13–15)
STUDY 3	Complete the personal study (pages 16–17)
CONNECT & DISCUSS	Connect with someone in your group (page 18)
CATCH UP & READ AHEAD (before week 2 group meeting)	Read chapters 4–6 in *When Your Way Isn't Working* Complete any unfinished personal studies (page 19)

DIAGNOSING DISCONNECTION

"I am the vine; you are the branches. If you remain in me and I in you, you will bear much fruit; apart from me you can do nothing."

JOHN 15:5

WELCOME |

It's not always easy for us to admit that our way isn't working. It's certainly never fun when someone who knows us well points this out and says, "Yeah, I don't think what you're doing is working so well." In those moments, we tend to feel more defensive than receptive.

Sometimes, we don't even realize that we *are* doing things our own way—and that our efforts are causing more problems than solutions. Other people might notice the fallout that we are leaving in our wake, but we still push forward, confidently trying to accomplish our goals and failing to see that we're trying to force a square peg into a round hole.

In this study, we will be looking at Jesus' answer to this problem. On the last night he spent with his disciples before he was crucified, he had a long talk with them about this very issue (see John 14–16). He was about to return to heaven, and though they didn't know it, they were about to be tasked with taking the gospel to the ends of the earth. Jesus knew if they tried to do it their own way, they would fail. Connected to him, though, they would bear much fruit.

So, yes, it doesn't feel great to admit that we're doing things wrong. But being honest in admitting our need is the first step toward a genuinely fruitful life. When we become willing to stop our efforts and acknowledge that we need God, we're ready for him to show us his way.

CONNECT | 15 MINUTES

If any of your group members don't know each other, take a few minutes to introduce yourselves. Then, to get things started, discuss one of the following questions:

- What is your primary goal or hope for participating in this study? (In other words, why are you here?)

  — *or* —

- What is something you are currently doing that is causing you to feel tired, worn out, or discouraged?

WATCH | 20 MINUTES

Now watch the video for this session, which you can access by playing the DVD or through streaming (see the instructions provided on the inside front cover). As you watch, use the following outline to record any concepts that stand out to you.

OUTLINE

  I. Sometimes we're the last to see it when our way isn't working.
   A. When someone confronts us, we usually get defensive or dismissive.
   B. Maybe our friends can see better than we can that our way just isn't working.
   C. Many of us don't like to admit our struggles—but that approach only works for so long.

 II. We need to ask for help and reprioritize our connection with Jesus and with people in our lives.
   A. Being honest about what's not working in our lives is not whining; it's actually being courageous.
   B. When we open up about what's hard, it leads to a question: *How's that working for you?*
   C. We need to evaluate our relationships, health, habits, and walk with God.

III. Jesus' words in John 15 to his disciples can help us when our way isn't working.
   A. Jesus knows our uncertainties, challenges, and weaknesses—and that our way doesn't work.
   B. He is the vine and we are the branches. When we are with him, we will bear fruit.
   C. But trying to bear fruit apart from Jesus is like watering a fake plant and expecting it to grow.
   D. Doing things our own way is frustrating and futile.

 IV. Jesus boils our need down to one word: *connection*.
   A. When our way isn't working, there's always a connection issue.
   B. We are branches, and a branch's most important job is to stay connected to the vine.
   C. We want to fix and control things with our to-do lists; we put production over connection.
   D. Connecting with Jesus begins when we recognize our need and humbly depend on him.

NOTES

DISCUSS | 35 MINUTES

Now discuss what you just watched by answering the following questions.

1. When have you tried hard to accomplish something but haven't succeeded? How did that make you feel? How did it affect your relationships, your job, or other aspects of your life?

2. How do you respond when someone tells you that he or she sees something in your life that might need changing? Why do you think you respond this way?

3. What would you say are some obvious signs that a person may not be closely connected to Jesus? What are some behaviors you exhibit when you aren't staying close to the Lord?

4. When have you witnessed the truth of Jesus' words in John 15:5—"Apart from me you can do nothing"? How did that reality make you feel?

5. Consider this statement from the teaching: "When your way isn't working, check your connection to the vine. You're the branch, and the branch's most important job is to just stay connected." How does this help explain what Jesus said in John 15:5?

RESPOND | 10 MINUTES

Sometimes, we don't even realize that we're doing things our own way and not God's way. However, a good way to tell is when we are constantly worn out, frustrated, irritable, discouraged, or battling other negative feelings. Thankfully, when our way isn't working, all we need to do is acknowledge our need and turn to Jesus. So take a few minutes on your own to consider whether or not your way is working, and then answer the questions below.

What spoke most to your heart from the video teaching?

What is God stirring you to do as a result?

How will this strengthen your connection to Jesus?

PRAY | 10 MINUTES

Praying for one another is one of the most important things you can do as a community. So use this prayer time wisely, and make it more than just a "closing prayer" to end your group experience. Be intentional about sharing your prayer requests, reviewing how God is answering your prayers, and praying for each other as a group. As you pray, ask God to show you where you might be doing things your own way and to teach you how to connect with him instead. Before you close your session, use the space below to write down any requests so that you and your group members can continue to pray about them in the week ahead.

Name   Request

PERSONAL STUDY

As you heard in this week's group time, sometimes we're the last ones to realize that our way isn't working all too well. After all, who of us likes to hear that we might need to consider making some changes in our lives? This week, you will have the chance to look at a few verses to see what the Bible says about why our own way doesn't work. As you consider these passages, ask God to show you exactly what he wants you to hear from him. He has something specific for you to take away from this study! As you work through the exercises, be sure to write down your responses to the questions, as you will be given a few minutes to share your insights at the start of the next session if you are doing this study with others. If you are reading *When Your Way Isn't Working* alongside this study, first review chapters 1–3 in the book.

THE PROBLEM CAN'T BE ME

None of us likes to be confronted. When a spouse or friend says, "Hey, you've been really touchy lately," it doesn't exactly make us happy. We might even think that the person who had the courage to speak to us is the real problem. It couldn't be us.

But when the individual confronting us is someone who has our best interests in mind, it's probably a good idea to listen. As a wise man once wrote, "Wounds from a friend can be trusted" (Proverbs 27:6). We just might realize that the person confronting us is right: *something we're doing isn't working.*

If you asked the people closest to you what they see in your life right now, what would they say? Maybe they would say you are distracted and irritable. Maybe they would say you have no time lately for family and friends. Maybe they would remark you seem discouraged or depressed or disconnected. Behaviors like this are symptoms of an underlying problem.

Even those who seem "spiritually together" need to be confronted at times. King David was once called out by the prophet Nathan after he had committed adultery with Bathsheba and had her husband killed. When Nathan confronted David, the king thought he was talking about someone else. So Nathan had to get direct: "You are the man!" (2 Samuel 12:7). We need to come to the same realization and be honest about our own problem areas.

It takes courage to acknowledge that our way isn't working. But it's the first step in the process of getting to a place where things *do* work. If we are willing to allow God to search our hearts, he will set us on the path toward a renewed life.

Read | Proverbs 27:5-6; 2 Samuel 12:1-25; and Proverbs 3:5-6

REFLECT

1. When has someone you loved and trusted confronted you about something in your life that he or she thought needed your attention? Which words from Proverbs 27:5–6 best describe your friend's actions?

> I think it's hard for me to ask for help because I don't like to be perceived as weak and I worry that asking for help comes off as whiny. If there is one thing I have a hard time with, it's grown adults, especially men, who whine. I even have a Bible verse for that—Philippians 2:14: "Do everything without grumbling or arguing." . . . That approach worked really well for me—until it didn't.[1]

2. How good are you at asking for help—or admitting that you need help in the first place? Who are two or three people in your life whom you could trust to steer you straight when your way isn't working?

3. Take a moment to review 2 Samuel 12:1–25. What story did Nathan tell David when he came to confront him? Why do you think he used a story?

The David was able to look at the issue more objectively when he thought the guilty person was someone else

I wanted to tell him my life felt out of control, like I was always under water, straining to break through the surface and get a lungful of air. I wanted to tell him I wasn't sleeping well at night because I couldn't turn off the scrolling list of things in my head that I hadn't gotten done that day. I wanted to tell him I felt lonely and that I hadn't been making time for the people closest to me. I wanted to tell him I hadn't been walking as closely with Jesus as I'd like to and how much I missed Jesus. I wanted to admit that the way I was living wasn't working, but I didn't say any of those things. Instead, I began to blame people and circumstances over which I had no control.[2]

4. How is the response in the quote above like David's initial response to Nathan's story? When have you responded to confrontation in a similar way? How did David respond after Nathan nailed him with the truth (see 2 Samuel 12:5–6, 13)?

He repented,

5. God tells us the truth not to hurt us but to help us. What three things does Proverbs 3:5–6 tell us to do? What does it say that God will do for us when we obey?

Trust the Lord
To NOT rely on our own insight or understanding.
Acknowledge Him

Pray | End your time in prayer. Ask God to help you be humble and open to what he wants to say to you in this study.

HOW'S THAT WORKING FOR YOU?

So maybe you're open to the idea that you haven't been handling things so well in your life. Deep down, you know that you're not living a fruitful life. But what can you do about it?

You can start by getting honest. This might mean taking an afternoon off to journal your thoughts. It might mean sharing with a trusted friend over coffee the load you've been carrying in your heart and mind. It might even mean talking with a counselor. However you do it, you need to take a square look at what's driving your choices and emotions.

A lot of us like to handle things on our own. We don't want to complain. We don't want to look weak or to bother people. And we really don't want others in our personal business. But maybe an independent mindset is what got us into trouble in the first place. Getting honest is not complaining, being weak, or burdening others with our issues. It's actually courageous.

When we first open up about our tiredness, discouragement, or fear, we feel vulnerable. At that point, it's easy to get defensive and blame others for our problems. But that response just proves that our need is greater than we think.

So, ask yourself today . . . *How's your way working?* What is it producing in your family, job, friendships, and walk with Jesus? If you don't like the answers, look at the way you've been living, and then let God show you a better way.

Read | Joshua 1:9 and Psalm 139

REFLECT

1. How hard is it for you to admit to yourself or others that your way isn't working? Why do you think this might be the case?

> Before I knew what was happening, I started to unload. . . . When I was finished, I was immediately ashamed. My wife would have been proud of me for being vulnerable, but I was sure I sounded weak and pathetic, probably whiny—although at some point, I definitely started to sound more annoyed. I have this thing I do where instead of vulnerably admitting that things are hard and I need help, I act annoyed. I say annoyed, but some people might say angry, but even angry seems better than whiny. It feels more powerful and less helpless.[3]

2. When you open up to someone about your struggles, you afterward might feel ashamed and regret having shared. How do God's words in Joshua 1:9 encourage you to be honest with others when the Lord is prompting you to do so?

> *How is your way working for you?* That question may be too general, so let me get a bit more specific. Take a few minutes to think through your answers to these questions:
>
> • Would the people you're closest to say that when they talk to you, you listen well?
> • Is it difficult to fall asleep at night? Do you wake up feeling lethargic?
> • How do you spend the first fifteen minutes of your morning?
> • What's the last thing you do before going to bed at night?

- What's the last passage of Scripture you read and meditated on? . . .
- Are you having a difficult time keeping commitments?
- How many unread or unanswered texts do you have right now?
- If you're a parent, can you tell me the names of your child's teachers?
- Have you been more irritable and easily annoyed with people? . . .
- How often do you say you're too busy when asked to do something you want to do?
- How often do you volunteer or find ways to serve every month?[4]

3. These questions can help you break down the broader question, *How's that working for you?* Choose one of the questions in this list to answer, and then write down your response below.

4. Being open about our needs helps us clearly admit that our way isn't working. When has honestly stating your problems been a help and relief to you?

5. When we get honest about what's going on in our lives, we need to remember that only God really knows our hearts. Take a few minutes to ask God to search your heart, as David did in Psalm 139. Ask him to help you see what he sees. Write what he shows you below.

Pray | End your time in prayer. Thank God that he knows your heart and can handle whatever burdens you've been carrying.

BE THE BRANCH

The night before Jesus was crucified, he had dinner with his disciples. Knowing he was about to leave them, he told them how to bear fruit after he was gone: "I am the vine; you are the branches. If you remain in me and I in you, you will bear much fruit; apart from me you can do nothing" (John 15:5). But what did Jesus mean by "remain in me"?

Well, what does a branch do? It just *is*. As long as it's attached to the vine, it bears fruit. It doesn't have to *do* anything. When it is disconnected from the vine, however, it won't produce a thing. (Sort of like the plastic plant a lady pointlessly watered for two years.)

To bear fruit, all we need to do is remain in Jesus—to stay connected to him. Some versions of the Bible translate "remain" as "abide." One version translates it as "stay joined." The same Greek word in other places is translated as "dwell," "live," or "continue." Basically, the point is that we need to live in Jesus. We need to be the branch. It's that simple.

Connected to Jesus, we will operate from a place of rest. Our impossible to-do lists, on the other hand, make us exhausted and exasperated. Psalm 127:2 says it well: "In vain you rise early and stay up late, toiling for food to eat—for he grants sleep to those he loves." Jesus was clear: "Apart from me you can do nothing." When we live in him, we bear much fruit.

Read | John 15:5; Psalm 127:1–2; and Colossians 2:6–7

REFLECT

1. What metaphor did Jesus give his disciples in John 15:5 to help them understand that they needed to stay connected to him? What is the branch's one job?

2. In what ways does Psalm 127:1–2 expand on what Jesus said in John 15:5?

3. What does it mean to stay connected to Jesus (see Colossians 2:6–7)? What are some things you can do to remain in him or stay connected to him?

4. According to the apostle Paul's words in Colossians 2:6–7, what are some of the results of living in Jesus?

5. Which words from Psalm 127:1–2 and John 15:5 best describe your life? Which words from these verses would you *like* to describe your life?

Pray | End your time in prayer. Ask God to help you stop struggling and striving to produce fruit and instead learn to remain in him.

CONNECT
& DISCUSS

Take some time today to connect with a group member and talk about some of the insights from this first session. Use the prompts below to guide your discussion.

What is one new thing you learned this week about staying connected to Jesus?

Which of the items in the list in study #2 most convicted you? Why?

What changes do you want to see as you become more connected to Jesus?

What can you change in your daily routine to help you better connect to Jesus?

How did the studies this week challenge you to draw closer to the Lord?

What else do you hope to gain as you go through this study?

CATCH UP &
READ AHEAD

Use this time to go back and complete any of the study and reflection questions from previous days that you weren't able to finish. Make a note below of any questions you've had, and reflect on any growth or personal insights you've gained.

Read chapters 4–6 in *When Your Way Isn't Working* before the next group session. Use the space below to make note of anything that stands out to you or encourages you from your reading.

WEEK 2

BEFORE GROUP MEETING	Read chapters 4–6 in *When Your Way Isn't Working* Read the Welcome section (page 23)
GROUP MEETING	Discuss the Connect questions Watch the video teaching for session 2 Discuss the questions that follow as a group Do the closing exercise and pray (pages 23–28)
STUDY 1	Complete the personal study (pages 30–32)
STUDY 2	Complete the personal study (pages 33–35)
STUDY 3	Complete the personal study (pages 36–37)
CONNECT & DISCUSS	Connect with someone in your group (page 38)
CATCH UP & READ AHEAD (before week 3 group meeting)	Read chapters 7–8 in *When Your Way Isn't Working* Complete any unfinished personal studies (page 39)

THE WHEEL OF EMOTIONS

Simon answered, "Master, we've worked hard all night and haven't caught anything. But because you say so, I will let down the nets."

LUKE 5:5

WELCOME |

In the first session of this study, we talked about the need for us to evaluate our lives and diagnose any disconnection that we may be experiencing in our relationship with Christ. Since Jesus is the vine, and we are the branches, our main job is to stay connected to him. When we are not protecting this connection with Jesus, things never really work out the way that they should.

In fact, when we are doing things our own way, it produces unhealthy results. One of those results that show up in our lives is negative emotions. Some of us are less emotional than others, of course, but anyone who is trying to do things without Jesus will end up feeling out-of-sorts one way or another. This is because we've stopped being the branch and are trying to be the vine. We're trying to find the answer in ourselves, and that just doesn't produce fruit.

In this session, we're going to look at four emotions that generally show up when we're trying to be productive apart from Jesus—and how those emotions can be warning signals that we need to check our connection with Christ. In this regard, Peter will serve as a great example of a person who needed help with his emotions. We're going to see how he handled it when Jesus wanted him to stop doing things his own way and instead let Christ take the lead.

If you are harassed by emotions that produce turmoil inside you or bring you down, the Lord wants to encourage you this week to bring those to him and find the peace and joy that come from union with him.

CONNECT | 15 MINUTES

Take a few minutes to get better acquainted with fellow members. Then choose one of the following questions to discuss as a group:

- What is something that spoke to your heart in last week's personal study that you would like to share with the group?

  — or —

- When have your emotions shown you that something was off in your life?

23

WATCH | 20 MINUTES

Now watch the video for this session. Below is an outline of the key points covered during the teaching. Record any key concepts that stand out to you.

OUTLINE

I. Identifying the emotions that we are feeling in the moment can help us better understand where they're coming from.
   A. Some of us define our emotions only as far as the word *fine*.
   B. But when we can identify our true feelings, we can better navigate where they will take us and how they will affect the people around us.
   C. When our way isn't working, certain emotions show up in our lives.

II. Peter wasn't always good at identifying and navigating his emotions.
   A. When Peter came back from a night of catching no fish (see Luke 5:3), his way clearly wasn't working.
   B. Peter seemed reluctant to follow Jesus' command to go back out. After all, he was a professional fisherman, and he hadn't succeeded in fishing.
   C. We are like Peter: we try hard to do well, but we don't always get the results that we want.

III. Four emotions typically show up when our way isn't working.
   A. **Discouragement** is a loss of confidence and enthusiasm.
   B. **Fatigue** is extreme physical and mental tiredness that comes from a prolonged period of concentrated exertion.
   C. **Frustration** is feeling upset or annoyed, especially because of an inability to change or achieve something.
   D. **Anxiety** is a feeling of worry or unease, typically when facing an imminent event or an uncertain outcome that we have no control over.

IV. When we're feeling these emotions—discouragement, fatigue, frustration, and anxiety—how should we respond?
   A. In Peter's case, he was tired and didn't want to go fishing again.
   B. However, even though Jesus' command didn't seem to make sense, Peter obeyed—and witnessed such a large catch the nets began to break.
   C. Obeying Jesus when we don't feel like it takes humble submission.
   D. But we can be assured that when Jesus is with us, we will bear much fruit.

NOTES

DISCUSS | 35 MINUTES

Now discuss what you just watched by answering the following questions.

1. Whether or not you think much about your feelings, your emotions can reveal a lot about what's going on inside your heart. When have your emotions let you know that something might be off in your life?

2. When have you put a lot of effort into something, only to find that it wasn't working? How did it feel at that point?

3. Ask someone in the group to read aloud Luke 5:1–10. Jesus, who wasn't a fisherman, told Peter, the expert fisherman, to go back out after a long night of catching nothing and let down his nets again. How would you have felt if you were in Peter's position? Why?

4. What are you especially good at? How much do you tend to depend on your own experience or expertise rather than let Jesus control your circumstances?

5. Consider this statement from the teaching: "Peter gives the only response that is the right response when your way isn't working: 'Because you say so, we'll let down the nets.'" When have you said yes to Jesus when you didn't feel like it? What was the result?

RESPOND | 10 MINUTES

It is disheartening when we try to accomplish a goal but end up with nothing to show for our efforts—especially when we're trying to do something positive like mend a friendship, strengthen a marriage, or succeed in our work. In times like these, our emotions can get the best of us. But Jesus' way *always* works. Take a few minutes on your own to think about what emotions might be flashing in your life right now, and then answer the questions below.

What spoke most to your heart from the video teaching?

What is God stirring you to do as a result?

How will this strengthen your connection to Jesus?

People used to Go to work because they had to to feed their families. They didn't have the luxury or inclination to let their feeling decide what they would do. They did however develop 27 a rhythm to life and were content in it. And often happier. ✗ rhythm

PRAY | 10 MINUTES

End your time by praying together as a group. As you pray, ask God to help you be honest about how your emotions might indicate a need to check your connection with him. Ask if anyone has prayer requests, and write those requests in the space below so you and your group members can continue to pray about them in the week ahead.

Name   Request

SESSION

15 "I am^a the true vine,^{b} and my Father is the gardener. 2He cuts that hears no fruit

TWO

PERSONAL STUDY

As we heard in this week's teaching, emotions typically show up in our lives when we are not staying connected to Jesus. This week, you will have the chance to look at a few verses to see what the Bible says about some of these emotions and how they can warn us to stop doing things our own way and instead follow Jesus' lead. As you work through the exercises, again write down your responses to the questions, as you will be given a few minutes to share your insights at the start of the next session if you are doing this study with others. If you are reading *When Your Way Isn't Working* alongside this study, first review chapters 4–6 in the book.

BECAUSE YOU SAY SO

When it comes to emotions, there is one person in the Bible who especially stands out: *Peter*. This disciple swung from fierce devotion to Jesus, to fearful denial of him, to heartbroken weeping over his own failure. He definitely displayed some turbulent emotions in his life.

The Bible doesn't tell us how Peter felt when he came back from a fruitless night of fishing. But as Jesus stepped onto his boat and began teaching the crowds, the weariness of a long night's work surely weighed on the fisherman.

We see evidence of this in Peter's response when Jesus asked him to put back out into the deep water, and let down the nets for a catch. "Master," Peter said, "we've worked hard all night and haven't caught anything" (Luke 5:4-5).

Peter knew a thing or two about fishing, after all. But Jesus didn't sympathize with Peter. He just waited for Peter to obey.

Despite his feelings, Peter yielded: "Because you say so, I will let down the nets" (verse 5). "Because you say so." It takes humble submission to say this to the Lord. But if we want a close connection with Jesus, this is where it begins.

With Jesus now in the boat, Peter brought in so many fish that his boat began to sink. At this, he fell down and repented: "Go away from me, Lord; I am a sinful man!" (verse 8). When Jesus is in our "boat," our lives will also never be the same.

If we acknowledge that our way isn't working and say yes to him, no matter how we feel, he will produce his fruit in us.

Read | Luke 5:1-11 and 1 Peter 5:6-7

REFLECT

1. When you are tired, what emotions do you typically display? (How would your family answer this question about you?)

2. How did Jesus' command to Peter in Luke 5:4 seem to overlook his tiredness? Why do you think it sometimes feels that God is unsympathetic to our feelings?

It turns out that in any area of your life that doesn't seem to be working, Jesus knows more than you think. He knows more about your job than you do. He knows more about your spouse than you do. He knows more about your children than you do. He knows more about your body than you do. He knows more about your finances than you do. He knows more about you than you do. So as you restart your journey with Jesus, the only way is to commit to humble submission. *That's* where connection begins.[5]

3. When has God asked you to do something that you didn't feel like doing or made no sense to you in the moment? How did you respond? How could the words of 1 Peter 5:6–7 help you trust God when his way doesn't make sense to you?

"Because you say so . . ." Considering some of the emotions that show up when our way isn't working, I want us to keep in mind that the only right response is, "Because you say so." Remember that emotions are always trying to *move* us somewhere, but Peter's response to Jesus is what moves him more than the way he's feeling in the moment. . . . *I'm tired and worn-out, but . . . because you say so. I really don't think this is going to work, but . . . because you say so. I don't feel like it, but . . . because you say so.*[6]

4. Who do you know who is more moved by Jesus than by his or her emotions? How does this person's example help you want to yield to God in the same way?

5. What was the final result of Jesus telling Peter to go back out fishing and causing him to catch so many fish (see Luke 5:11)? What kind of fruit do you think this produced in Peter's life—and also throughout the history of the church?

Pray | End your time in prayer. Ask God to give you a humble, trusting heart that will tell him "because you say so," no matter how you feel or what he asks of you.

STAND UP

Whenever we stop being the branch and try to be the vine, certain emotions will begin to build up inside us. One is *discouragement*.

A woman in the Old Testament named Hannah understood this emotion only all too well. She had no child, while her husband's other wife, Peninnah, produced multiple children. What's worse, Peninnah constantly mocked her for it.

Hannah was so anguished that she wept and would not eat. Her experience could be the definition of discouragement, for we read in the story that "this went on year after year" (1 Samuel 1:7). Most of us can handle disappointment for a while. But when that disappointment goes on *year after year*, we lose hope, confidence, and courage.

On one occasion, during the family's annual journey to the tabernacle in Shiloh, the Bible tells us that "Hannah stood up" (verse 9). Those words, "stood up," speak of more than just physical posture. Hannah was through with carrying all her pain. She was finally desperate enough to stand up and hand her grief over to God.

"In her deep anguish Hannah prayed to the Lord, weeping bitterly" (verse 10). She told the Lord that if he would give her a son, she would give him back to God. Hannah wasn't negotiating—she was surrendering. God didn't promise Hannah anything. But after praying, Hannah ate, and "her face was no longer downcast" (verse 18). She had reset her connection with God. (Later, God gave her a son, Samuel, whom Hannah indeed gave back to God.)

If your emotions signal a disconnection with Jesus, do what Hannah did at Shiloh and *stand up*. Pour out your heart to God. Your circumstances may not instantly change, but your discouragement will be replaced with Jesus' peace.

Read | 1 Samuel 1 and Hebrews 12:1–3

REFLECT

1. Discouragement sets in when what we experience is different from what we expected.[7] When has your experience been different from what you expected? How have you handled your disappointment?

> The closest thing I have to a superpower is the ability to always choose the longest line. Whether it's a checkout line, a drive-through, or the airport security line, I will always choose the longest line. . . .
>
> Here's what I know from years and years of experience at waiting in long lines: I don't get discouraged unless I compare. If I avoid tracking the speed of my line with the line next to me, everything is fine. If I compare, I become discouraged.
>
> The discouragement dial gets turned up when our way isn't working, but even more so when everyone else's way seems to be doing just fine.
>
> We can call this the "Peninnah effect." It's one thing to be barren; it's quite another thing to live in the same house with your husband's other wife who is popping out kids. It was especially difficult when they would travel as one big family to Shiloh and Peninnah would rub it in Hannah's face.[8]

2. How does it make your pain greater when you compare your circumstances to someone else's? How can Hebrews 12:1–3 help you in that regard?

3. What words in 1 Samuel 1:10–16 show Hannah's emotions? What words give you insight into her feelings after she poured out her grief and anguish to the Lord (see verses 17–18)?

> You reach a point where you've tried things your way. You've attempted to fix your problem, control it, ignore it, diminish it, and dismiss it. You've even allowed yourself to wallow in it. And now it's all led to a desperate moment when you have to decide if you'll keep sitting or if you'll stand up. Hannah stood up and went to pray.[9]

4. How did Hannah show by her actions that she had truly given up her own way and had chosen to embrace God's way (see 1 Samuel 1:24–28)?

5. How might God be stirring you to stand up—to be done with whatever discouragement, frustration, fatigue, or anxiety is weighing you down? Stand up. Pour out your heart to the Lord. Take a few minutes to do that right now!

Pray | End your time in prayer. Ask God to give you the strength to stand up and hand your burdens over to him.

HEED THE FLASHING LIGHTS

Most of us don't deliberately disconnect from Jesus. But if we consistently feel discouraged, frustrated, fatigued, or anxious, it should cause us to consider whose way we are following. Just like the warning lights on a car's dashboard, there are "warning lights" when it comes to our emotions that should tell us our way isn't working.

The *frustration* alert starts with mild irritation and escalates to annoyance, indignation, and eventually rage. The more frustrated we get with people, the less we are abiding in Jesus. Cain had a serious problem with this (see Genesis 4:1–12).

The *fatigue* alert starts when we don't have enough margin in our lives to stay deeply connected to Jesus and others. Fatigue can eventually bring us to despair. This is what happened to Elijah when he fled from the wrath of Queen Jezebel (see 1 Kings 19:1–5).

The *anxiety* alert shows up in fear, nervousness, irritability, and sleeplessness. It can include breathing difficulties, chest pain, headaches, and other physical problems. Anxiety often surfaces in agitation, anger, and annoyance. Moses showed some of these emotions when the Lord told him to lead God's people out of Egypt (see Exodus 4:1–17).

When we see these flashing lights, we should check if we've disconnected with Jesus. When Cain became angry, God asked him to examine himself (see Genesis 4:6). When Elijah's fatigue alarm was blaring, God helped him rest and reconnect (see 1 Kings 19:5–8). When Moses resisted God's direction, God simply told him, "I will be with you" (Exodus 3:12). Facing our emotions requires humility. But when we are willing to change, true connection can begin.

Read | Genesis 4:3-7; 1 Kings 19:1-8; and Exodus 3:10-14

REFLECT

1. When Cain was angry, what did God tell Cain to do (see Genesis 4:6-7)? How was this another way of telling Cain to humble himself and reconnect with God?

2. Why do you think Elijah was so depressed after his great victory on Mount Carmel (see 1 Kings 18:16-46)? When have you felt fatigued or down after a big high that you have experienced in your life?

3. How does God's first statement to Moses in Exodus 3:12 amplify what Jesus taught to his disciples in John 15:4-5? How can reconnecting with Jesus calm any anxiety that you may feel?

4. What are some practical ways that you can unplug from the busyness of life and get some rest in order to regain a quiet heart with Jesus?

5. What emotions are flashing on the dashboard of your life? What is God telling you to do about them—examine yourself, get some rest, relax in his presence, something else?

Pray | End your time in prayer. Ask God to help you identify any emotions that reveal a disconnection from him and to strengthen you to draw near to him again.

CONNECT
& DISCUSS

Take some time today to connect with a group member and talk about some of the insights from this second session. Use the prompts below to guide your discussion.

What surprised you as you thought about how your emotions reflect the state of your heart?

Of the four emotions discussed this week, which have you most experienced?

What is one indicator that you need to reset your connection with Jesus?

Which point of teaching this week most challenged you?

Which point of teaching from this week most encouraged and helped you?

If you had one prayer request based on this week's study, what would it be?

CATCH UP &
READ AHEAD

Use this time to go back and complete any of the study and reflection questions from previous days that you weren't able to finish. Make a note below of any questions you've had, and reflect on any growth or personal insights you've gained.

Read chapters 7-8 in *When Your Way Isn't Working* before the next group session. Use the space below to make note of anything that stands out to you or encourages you from your reading.

WEEK 3

BEFORE GROUP MEETING	Read chapters 7-8 in *When Your Way Isn't Working* Read the Welcome section (page 43)
GROUP MEETING	Discuss the Connect questions Watch the video teaching for session 3 Discuss the questions that follow as a group Do the closing exercise and pray (pages 43-48)
STUDY 1	Complete the personal study (pages 50-52)
STUDY 2	Complete the personal study (pages 53-55)
STUDY 3	Complete the personal study (pages 56-57)
CONNECT & DISCUSS	Connect with someone in your group (page 58)
CATCH UP & READ AHEAD (before week 4 group meeting)	Read chapters 9-10 in *When Your Way Isn't Working* Complete any unfinished personal studies (page 59)

THE WAY OF CONNECTION

"Remain in me, as I also remain in you."

JOHN 15:4

WELCOME | READ ON YOUR OWN

As we have seen, when we do things our own way, nothing works the way it should. Negative emotions surface, making it obvious to us—and everyone around us—that we aren't drawing our life from Jesus. Thankfully, the Lord uses our failed efforts and worn-out emotions to get our attention and draw us back to him so we can bear fruit.

Of course, the problem is often that when we think of bearing fruit, we don't think of connecting with Jesus. Instead, we think of *production*. We want to accomplish big works and then offer them up to God: "Look what I did! Now you'll be pleased with me!" But when we try to bear fruit by *doing* for God, we are doing things our own way. In our efforts to bear fruit, we miss out on a deep relationship with Jesus and end up with tired bodies, minds, and hearts.

In this session, we are going to look at what connection to Jesus really means. We are going to see that if we are going to stay close to Jesus, it has to start with us getting quiet, sitting down, and spending time with him. While this way of producing fruit seems counterintuitive to us—we don't *like* to be still and rest—the process of bearing fruit doesn't come by human effort. It comes from abiding in Jesus. Connection first, then production.

Only God can produce fruit. He wants us to get off the treadmill of our busy lives and sit down at his feet. He wants us to be still enough to allow his presence to flow into us and create the perfect conditions for fruit-bearing. As we connect more deeply with Jesus, his life *will* flow into us, and we will begin to see the fruit growing naturally in our lives.

CONNECT | 15 MINUTES

Get the session started by choosing one of the following questions to discuss together as a group:

- What is something that spoke to your heart in last week's personal study that you would like to share with the group?

  — *or* —

- When have you prioritized your to-do list over time with someone you love?

WATCH | 20 MINUTES

Now watch the video for this session. Below is an outline of the key points covered during the teaching. Record any key concepts that stand out to you.

OUTLINE

I. Jesus, on the night of his arrest, spoke to his disciples about production.
   A. Jesus knew they had a mission ahead of them to take the gospel to the world.
   B. We might think Jesus would lay out a five-year productivity plan or strategy.
   C. Instead, Jesus taught that connection with him is the way to production for him.

II. If the disciples remained in Christ, they would bear much fruit.
   A. Some believe Jesus' words prioritize fruit bearing—a "work harder" mentality.
   B. Production matters, but when we try to bear fruit in our efforts, it doesn't work.
   C. Jesus showed his disciples a vine and its branches and said, "You be the branch."

III. We may prioritize production over connection to earn approval and reward.
   A. We are taught from the time we are young that results get rewarded.
   B. We may grow up in homes where affection was given based on accomplishments.
   C. God doesn't withhold relationship from us until we produce enough to earn it.
   D. God's way is the opposite: production flows out of connection.

IV. We may prioritize production over connection because we can measure it.
   A. Production can be tracked and gives us a feeling of accomplishment.
   B. Production is visible; it enables us to compare what we've done to how much others have done.

V. The story of Mary and Martha in Luke 10:38–42 reveals how we should prioritize connection over production.
   A. When Jesus and his disciples came to the home of Martha and Mary, we read that Martha got busy with production.
   B. But Mary, the other sister, chose to sit at Jesus' feet and listen to him teach—which made Martha irritated.
   C. Jesus noticed this and told Martha, "Mary has chosen what is better, and it will not be taken away from her" (verse 42).
   D. Production matters, but it needs to come from connection. Which one are you putting first?

NOTES

We hav

DISCUSS | 35 MINUTES

Now discuss what you just watched by answering the following questions.

1. What do you tend to put first—production *for* Jesus or connection *with* him? What are a few examples of some of the things you tend to put first in your life?

Henri Nouwen Quote.

2. Ask someone in the group to read aloud Ephesians 2:8–10. What does this passage say about works? Why is it critical for us to remember that we are saved by our faith and God's grace?

3. Consider this statement from the teaching: "The challenge for most of us is that when our way isn't working, we instinctively want to double down on production and make it happen out of our own strength and determination." Have you found this to be true in your life? Why do you think we keep trying to bear fruit ourselves even when our way isn't working?

4. Take a moment to review Luke 10:38–42. How would you describe Martha's state of mind in this passage? Why did Jesus say her sister, Mary, had chosen what was better?

5. Would you say that you tend to be more like Martha, who was distracted with preparations, or more like Mary, who sat at the feet of Jesus? If you feel that you are more like Martha in the story, in what ways could you be less distracted with work and more focused on Jesus?

RESPOND | 10 MINUTES

Jesus wants us to bear much fruit. The thing we need to remember is that bearing fruit doesn't come first. Abiding in Jesus, or staying connected to him, is the priority. When we set aside our own efforts to be fruitful and learn to sit quietly at Jesus' feet, we will find peace and rest. Take a few minutes on your own to consider some ways in which you might be prioritizing production over connection with Jesus, and then answer the questions below.

What spoke most to your heart from the video teaching?

What is God stirring you to do as a result?

How will this strengthen your connection to Jesus?

PRAY | 10 MINUTES

End your time by praying together as a group. As you pray, ask God to show you ways in which you might be trying to gain his approval or impress others with your work for him. Ask the Lord to help you exchange those ways for connection with him and the fruit that only he can produce in you. Ask if anyone has prayer requests, and write those in the space below so that you and your group members can continue to pray about them in the week ahead.

Name	Request

PERSONAL STUDY

As you heard on this week's teaching, Jesus wants us to bear fruit, but he wants us to learn that this fruit comes not by our hard work but only by staying connected to him. This week, you will have the chance to look at a few verses to see what the Bible says about what it means to abide in Christ first so that you can bear fruit for him. As you work through the exercises, be sure to write down your responses to the questions, as you will be given a few minutes to share your insights at the start of the next session if you are doing this study with others. If you are reading *When Your Way Isn't Working* alongside this study, first review chapters 7–8 in the book.

WORK DOESN'T WORK

So far in this study, we have emphasized that doing things our way doesn't work. But what is it about our way that's the problem? Why *doesn't* our way lead to the life we desire?

In the Bible, our "way" is generally referred to as "work" (see, for example, Romans 4:4–5 and Hebrews 4:10). We work because it is wired into us to be independent and self-sufficient. We don't like to lean on others—it feels like weakness to us. We enjoy the feeling of accomplishment that hard work brings, and we work because we fear rejection. We try to please God in order to gain his favor. This idea of production is often associated with religion.

Hard work isn't bad. It's encouraged in Scripture (see 1 Timothy 6:18). It's good to do our jobs skillfully and honorably. But the do-it-yourself model isn't the way to a relationship with Jesus.

While our way is "work," Jesus' way is "rest." The great Methodist preacher Samuel Chadwick once wrote, "Works are by the sweat of man's brow; fruit is God's gift to man. Fruit does not come by toil but by appropriation, assimilation, and abiding."[10] Work doesn't produce fruit. After all, have you ever heard of a branch straining to produce an apple or a peach?

Fruit comes not from trying harder but by being still. When we live in Jesus, his life flows into us and the fruit we desire starts to grow effortlessly. Our striving gives way to life and joy that will bless both us and the people around us. So, if our MO is work, we need to remember that *work doesn't work*. We have only one job: be the branch.

Read | John 15:4–8; John 6:27–29; Romans 4:4–5; and Matthew 11:28–30

REFLECT

1. We tend to think that connection with God or others is something that must be earned. We subconsciously approach our relationship with God this way, thinking the best way to connect with him is through producing for him.[11] What is one area of your life in which you have tried hard to produce for God but have always seemed to come up short?

2. In John 6:27–29, Jesus tells us what the work of God is (see also Hebrews 4:10–11). Write verse 29 below. How is the work of God the same as abiding in the vine?

Bootstrapping refers to the ability to get ourselves out of a difficult situation or to make something happen without requiring external help or input. It appeals to our pride and ego. Being the branch implies a level of dependence and insufficiency that we are reluctant to admit to. . . . The truth is, the moment I admit weakness and ask for help, I can no longer wear the "DIY badge" with pride. Instead of being the person who made it happen, I'm the person who needed help to make it happen. Prioritizing connection over production is difficult for a bootstrapper who can't accept their own weakness or recognize that the do-it-yourself way of living isn't working.[12]

3. What are some examples of "pulling yourself up by your bootstraps" in your life? According to Romans 4:4–5, what do we receive when we abide (or trust) in God?

4. Jesus' words in Matthew 11:28–30 have comforted and strengthened many people over the centuries. How does this passage give insight into what work does to people? What alternative does Jesus offer to his followers?

> It's not that doing doesn't matter; it's that doing should flow from being. Being the branch, abiding in Christ, often doesn't feel like we're doing anything. But being connected always leads to fruitfulness in the most important ways.[13]

5. Jesus wants us to bear "much fruit" (John 15:8) by being the branch. As you reflect on this truth, how does it sit with you? Do you find that abiding in Jesus, the vine, seems like you "aren't doing anything"? What tends to get in the way of you spending time with God?

Pray | End your time in prayer. Ask God to help you not to work to try to please him but instead to abide in him and draw your life and strength from him.

CONNECTION COMES FIRST

Life is short. If we want to live fruitful lives, we've got to put first things first. As we've noted, we often put production ahead of connection. We chase after careers and run to one activity after another, until one day we suddenly realize, "Where did all the time go?" But God calls us to connection before production—first with Jesus, and then with other people.[14]

When Jesus called his disciples, he "appointed twelve that they might be with him and that he might send them out to preach" (Mark 3:14).

Notice the order. The disciples were first to *be with Jesus*, and then they were to serve. For three years the disciples watched, listened, and asked questions. Being with Christ prepared them to take the gospel to the world.[15]

How do we connect with Jesus? By spending time with him. By quieting our hearts before him. By asking him to speak to us by his Spirit through his Word.

Praying. Listening. Adoring. Obeying.

Abiding is much more than just believing the truth about Jesus. It is cultivating the habit of living in Christ, not only in quiet times with him, but all day, every day. Life goes by quickly. Steward it well. Production is temporary, but connection is eternal.

Read | Mark 3:14; John 15:4-5; Psalm 39:4-6; and James 4:8

REFLECT

1. While we can't be with Jesus physically, like the twelve disciples were, we can be with Jesus by his Spirit, who lives within us. In what ways do you prioritize being with Jesus?

> Connection always feels like it can wait, but production feels like it needs to happen right now. . . . Connection often feels like something we can catch up on when things aren't so busy. We are going to start being more intentional to sit at the feet of Jesus, but now's just not a good time. And when we do try to spend some time connecting with him, we feel the pressure of what needs to be taken care of right away.[16]

2. Have you ever fallen into this way of thinking that connection is something you can "catch up on" later when things aren't so busy? What is the danger in thinking this way? What does Psalm 39:4–6 say about the importance of connection with Christ right now?

3. While God wants us to connect with him first, he also wants us to have fellowship with the people he has placed in our lives. With whom might God want you to spend more time in an intentional way? What can you do to start making that happen?

God does not want us to neglect our responsibilities or ignore our duties. He wants us to be good stewards of what he has entrusted to us. The challenge to us in this chapter is to prioritize our connections—first with Jesus and then with others—and then allow what our lives produce to flow from those connections.[17]

4. *God wants us to be good stewards of his resources.* What are some areas in your life that you would like to better steward the gifts that God has given to you? How would purposely being with Jesus—not just in a quiet time but throughout your day—enable you to bear more fruit?

5. The good news about connecting with Jesus is that it's never too late to start. Take a moment to review James 4:8. How does this promise in this verse motivate you to a fresh start?

Pray | End your time in prayer. Thank God that he wants you to be with him, and ask him to help you to want that too.

CHOOSING WHAT IS BETTER

When Jesus and his twelve disciples (and whoever else was with them) showed up on Martha and Mary's doorstep, it was Martha who invited them in. Her mind probably went into overdrive as she began calculating how she would feed her guests.

The crowd settled in, and Jesus began teaching. But Mary, instead of helping with the meal, "sat at the Lord's feet listening to what he said" (Luke 10:39). As we've seen, this irritated Martha, who complained about it to Jesus.

Jesus loved Martha, so he spoke to her clearly: "'Martha, Martha,' the Lord answered, 'you are worried and upset about many things, but few things are needed—or indeed only one. Mary has chosen what is better, and it will not be taken away from her'" (verses 41–42).

Martha put production first. Her motives were good, but her negative emotions were flashing signals that her way wasn't working. Mary put connection first. Her longing to be with Jesus overrode any pressure that she might have felt to help Martha.

So it was that when Jesus told Martha, "It will not be taken away from her," he meant that what Mary had chosen would last forever. Jesus similarly told his disciples, "I chose you and appointed you so that you might go and bear fruit—*fruit that will last*" (John 15:16, emphasis added).

What Mary had chosen was better because it was *eternal*. Busyness and stress kill our ability to just sit at the feet of Jesus and be with him. We need to stop our whirling thoughts and just rest in his presence. Will you commit to do that today?

Read | Luke 10:38–42; Matthew 6:19–20; John 15:16; and Psalm 127:1

REFLECT

1. Look again at the description of the two sisters. Mary "sat at the Lord's feet listening to what he said." Martha was "distracted by all the preparations" (Luke 10:39–40). Who would you say that you are more like—Martha or Mary? Explain.

2. What is your definition of *distractions*? What are some of the "distractions" you are chasing that might be making you feel stressed, anxious, or irritable? What steps can you take to move from being "worried and upset" about them to choosing "what is better"?

3. The kind of fruit that Jesus wants us to bear is "fruit that will last" (John 15:16). How do Christ's words in Matthew 6:19–20 motivate you to bear this kind of fruit?

4. According to Psalm 127:1, what are the results of doing things our own way, or putting production for Jesus ahead of connection with Jesus? What might you be trying to accomplish through your own "labor" that the Lord isn't building?

5. How does Mary's desire to sit at Jesus' feet inspire you to want to do the same thing? What does "sitting at the feet of Jesus" look like in your life?

Pray | End your time in prayer. Ask God to help you learn to sit at his feet so that you might bear fruit that will last.

CONNECT
& DISCUSS

Take some time today to connect with a group member and talk about some of the insights from this third session. Use the prompts below to guide your discussion.

What new insights about connecting with Jesus did you gain this week?

What is one way that you need to stop working for God and instead rest in him?

Which truth in this session most convicted your heart?

How will the reminder that life is short affect what you put first in your life?

What helped you the most in this session about putting connection over production?

What changes will you make in your daily life to help you better abide in Christ?

CATCH UP &
READ AHEAD

Use this time to go back and complete any of the study and reflection questions from previous days that you weren't able to finish. Make a note below of any questions you've had, and reflect on any growth or personal insights you've gained.

Read chapters 9–10 in *When Your Way Isn't Working* before the next group session. Use the space below to make note of anything that stands out to you or encourages you from your reading.

WEEK 4

BEFORE GROUP MEETING	Read chapters 9–10 in *When Your Way Isn't Working* Read the Welcome section (page 63)
GROUP MEETING	Discuss the Connect questions Watch the video teaching for session 4 Discuss the questions that follow as a group Do the closing exercise and pray (pages 63–68)
STUDY 1	Complete the personal study (pages 70–72)
STUDY 2	Complete the personal study (pages 73–75)
STUDY 3	Complete the personal study (pages 76–77)
CONNECT & DISCUSS	Connect with someone in your group (page 78)
CATCH UP & READ AHEAD (before week 5 group meeting)	Read chapters 11–12 in *When Your Way Isn't Working* Complete any unfinished personal studies (page 79)

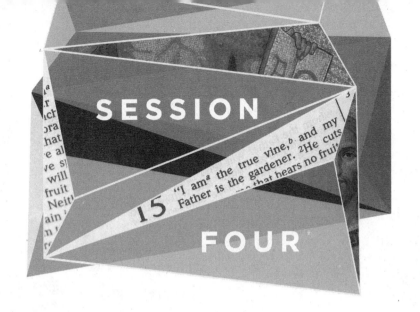

THE PURPOSE
OF PRUNING

*"My Father is the gardener. He [lifts up]
every branch in me that bears no fruit, while
every branch that does bear fruit he prunes
so that it will be even more fruitful."*

JOHN 15:1–2

WELCOME | READ ON YOUR OWN

In the previous session, we discussed the importance of connection over production. When we do things our own way by working hard instead of staying close to Jesus and drawing our life from him, we don't bear any fruit. This is why we need to make sure we're abiding in him.

But did you know that you can actually be connected to Christ and still not bear fruit? Jesus commented on this truth to his disciples when he said, "[God] cuts off every branch in me that bears no fruit" (John 15:2). Thankfully, Jesus also revealed how his heavenly Father, the Gardener, helps the unfruitful branches so they can begin to produce as they should.

The Gardener doesn't just deal with the branches that aren't bearing fruit. He also works on the branches that are already fruitful. In other words, he *prunes* them. While we might not like the idea that God will cut things from our lives that are bearing fruit, he wants us to be even *more* fruitful for him. Our Father, the Gardener, cuts off things in our lives that are slowing down the growth he wants to see in us. This is what we'll be looking at in this session.

Pruning is painful, but as anyone who has tended a garden knows, it's necessary for the health and fruitfulness of a plant. The fact that our Gardener is *God* ought to give us comfort, because he loves us and would never do anything to harm us. We can trust him when he prunes us because we know that he is working toward increased fruit in our lives—fruit that will last.

CONNECT | 15 MINUTES

Get the session started by choosing one of the following questions to discuss together as a group:

- What is something that spoke to your heart in last week's personal study that you would like to share with the group?

— *or* —

- When has something painful in your life turned out for good?

WATCH | 20 MINUTES

Now watch the video for this session. Below is an outline of the key points covered during the teaching. Record any key concepts that stand out to you.

OUTLINE

I. A gardener prunes with an intentional picture in mind.
   A. Do we trust the picture that God, the Gardener, has in mind?
   B. When our way isn't working, it's time for us to embrace the pruning God wants to do in us.
   C. The picture that God has in mind as he prunes us is *Jesus*.

II. Jesus said that God "cuts off every branch" in him that bears no fruit.
   A. Jesus taught that if we remain in him, we will bear fruit. But now he seems to say that if we don't bear fruit, he will cut us off. Which is it?
   B. The Greek word *airo*, translated "cuts off," can also be translated "lifts up."
   C. In a vineyard, when a branch falls to the ground, the gardener picks it up, cleans it off, and entwines it with other branches so it can produce again.
   D. God does the same for us. Moving from a "cut you off" theology to a "lift you up" theology will help us trust the Gardener.

III. Pruning isn't punishment.
   A. God prunes the branches that do bear fruit so that they will produce more.
   B. God removes the dead and diseased branches—the sin in our lives.
   C. God removes sucker branches—the distractions that don't produce fruit.
   D. God removes healthy branches—good things—for something even better.

IV. Pruning isn't pointless.
   A. Pruning feels pointless, but it always has a purpose: fruit that will last.
   B. Pruning hurts; the loss of our treasured things can make us feel frustrated.
   C. We need to wait and see. In time, God's purpose will be clear to us.

V. When your way isn't working, invite God into your life to do the pruning that needs to be done.
   A. Pruning is less painful when we pray for it than when God has to deal with us.
   B. If we resist God's pruning, we will become like dry sticks, useful only for the fire.
   C. Submit yourself to God, the good Gardener. He can be trusted.

NOTES

Sometimes we want to make sure everything in a loved ones
Life turns out as we think it should. We wish we could control
all the factors so that it would work out "Best."

However if we look back over our lives how many of
often did the things we changed turn out to be significant
would have
in the making us who we are today. How often would we
have hidden Gods pruning shears if we could have.

This World is a perfectly safe place to be.
                                                    D. W.

DISCUSS | 35 MINUTES

Now discuss what you just watched by answering the following questions.

1. Ask someone to read Romans 8:29. When God prunes us, he has a picture in mind of what he's shaping us to be. According to this verse, what is that picture? How does this shed light on what kind of fruit God wants to see in us?

2. How does it encourage you to know that God does not cut off a branch that doesn't bear fruit but instead picks it up so that it will become healthy again?

3. Consider these statements from the teaching: "Really, the question becomes, do you trust the picture? Do you trust the Gardener, who has the shears, that he's going to make it beautiful, that he's going to make it grow, that it's going to be better when he's done with it than it was before he started?" How would you answer each of these questions?

4. What are the different kinds of branches that God prunes in our lives? What is one particular "sucker branch" that he may want to cut off in your life?

5. Ask someone in the group to read 1 Peter 5:6. Why is it important for us to submit ourselves to God's pruning process? What is the promise when we humble ourselves before God?

66

RESPOND | 10 MINUTES

It hurts to have things cut off in our lives, especially when those things seem good and healthy to us. But God is after something better for us: he wants to shape us into the image of Jesus, his Son. We can trust the Gardener because he is working to make us as fruitful as possible. So take a few minutes on your own as you close this session to think about anything that God may want to prune from your life, and then answer the questions below.

What spoke most to your heart from the video teaching?

What is God stirring you to do as a result?

How will this strengthen your connection to Jesus?

PRAY | 10 MINUTES

End your time by praying together as a group. As you pray, ask God to make you open to the pruning that he wants to do in your life and to help you trust him in the process. Ask if anyone has prayer requests, and write those requests in the space below so you and your group members can continue to pray about them in the week ahead.

Name   Request

PERSONAL STUDY

As you heard in the teaching this week, God removes certain things from our lives so we will bear fruit—and *more* fruit. This week, you will look at a few verses to see what the Bible says about the way in which God, the "Gardener," prunes his people, the "branches," and how this enables good fruit to be produced in us. As you work through the exercises, be sure to write down your responses to the questions, as you will be given a few minutes to share your insights at the start of the next session if you are doing this study with others. If you are reading *When Your Way Isn't Working* alongside this study, first review chapters 9–10 in the book.

YOU CAN TRUST THE GARDENER

When Jesus said that he is the vine and we are the branches, he also talked about someone else: his Father, the Gardener. As he said, "I am the true vine, and my Father is the gardener" (John 15:1). But the statement that Jesus then makes to his disciples about God's gardening methods has caused anxiety for many Christians: "He cuts off every branch in me that bears no fruit" (verse 2).

So, does this mean that if we don't bear fruit . . . God will *cut us off*? Is this the true meaning of what Jesus is saying by making this statement?

The answer may be found in looking at what a gardener does in our world. When a gardener has a beautiful tree or vine that isn't producing, his first inclination isn't to chop it down. Rather, he looks for the problem. *Is the tree sick? Does it need fertilizer? Is it crowded by other bushes? If it's a grapevine, have the branches fallen into the dirt?*

As you heard in this week's teaching, the word translated "cuts off" in John 15:2 can also mean "lifts up."[18] Using that translation gives this verse a completely different meaning: "He *lifts up* every branch in me that bears no fruit." Suddenly, what Jesus is saying in this verse becomes encouraging!

Yes, we should be bearing fruit. If we aren't, it *does* indicate that there is a problem. But we don't have to fear that God is going to come along and lop us off. No, our God picks us up, cleans us off, and intertwines us with stronger branches for support.[19] We can trust the Gardener. If we are humble and correctable, then we will become the fruitful branches that he wants us to be.

Read | John 15:1-2; Luke 15:11-24; and Micah 7:18-19

REFLECT

1. Jesus tells us that "[God] *lifts up* every branch in me that bears no fruit." How does that alternate reading for John 15:2 help you to better understand God's purpose as a gardener in your life?

When we think about what we have done or have not done, we tend to assume that God is a vengeful gardener with a machete in hand, ready to lop off any branch that isn't producing enough fruit. We try to be good enough to keep God from snapping, but we're not sure what the standard for "good enough" is. Thus we spend our lives oscillating between self-righteousness (because we think we've met the standard) and shame (because we're certain that we've fallen short).

I truly believe that God loves me, forgives me, and has saved me from my sin. I know that those things are true, but if I'm honest, I sometimes feel that God is frustrated with me. I feel like he barely tolerates me and if I don't start producing some serious fruit, he's going to cut me off. You've felt that too? This subtle but malignant misunderstanding of God probably stems from a different place for every person. . . . [But] ultimately, the real source of this is an enemy who wants to convince you that you have been ghosted by God and that he is going to cut you off.[20]

2. When you think of yourself as a branch and God as the Gardener, does that image encourage you or does it make you nervous? Why do you feel this way?

3. While it might be hard to evaluate your own life, how fruitful would you say you are? In what ways might God need to pick you up, clean you off, lift you back into the air and light, and intertwine you with stronger branches (other believers)?

> The gardener's goal is to *airo* [lift up] withering branches so that their connection can be strengthened and fruit can begin to grow. When it's clear that your way hasn't worked for you and you find yourself covered in dirt and surrounded by weeds, there is a gardener with a graceful heart and gentle hands who longs to pick you up.[21]

4. Review the story of the prodigal son in Luke 15:11–24. How does this parable reflect the picture of God as a gardener picking up a fallen branch so it might be fruitful again?

5. The prophet Micah reminded the Israelites—who found themselves in exile as a result of their idolatrous practices against God—that he would not "stay angry forever" at them but would "delight to show mercy" to them (Micah 7:18). How does this encourage you today?

Pray | End your time in prayer. Ask God to lift you up and make you fruitful, and thank him that you can trust him as a good gardener.

PRUNING IS NOT PUNISHMENT

When difficult or painful circumstances come our way, we might think that God is punishing us for a wrong that we have done against him. But the truth is that God also allows hard things in our lives because he *loves* us. Jesus said it this way: "Every branch that does bear fruit he prunes so that it will be even more fruitful" (John 15:2).

God prunes three kinds of branches. First, he cuts off *dead and diseased* branches. This represents our sinful behaviors. Even when we are bearing fruit in some areas of our lives, we can still struggle with deep-seated destructive habits or hidden sins.

Second, God cuts off *sucker* branches. These are things that suck the life the fruit-bearing branches need. Sucker branches represent things that aren't necessarily bad—social media, activities, hobbies—but can weaken our connection to Jesus.

Third, God cuts off *healthy* branches. This one is hard for us to understand. We lose a job, or have to let go of a goal, or don't see a dream realized. We don't think of healthy branches like these as something that God needs to cut back. But in the end, he does this kind of pruning so that something even greater can grow in its place.

The bottom line is that when God prunes us, it isn't because he is punishing us. As we read in Hebrews 12:7-8, "Endure hardship as discipline; God is treating you as his children. For what children are not disciplined by their father? If you are not disciplined—and everyone undergoes discipline—then you are not legitimate, not true sons and daughters at all." When your way isn't working, God may be pruning something from your life to make you more fruitful—and more like Christ.

Read | John 15:1–2; Colossians 3:1-17; and Hebrews 12:5-13

REFLECT

1. When have you been surprised by God removing something that you saw as healthy from your life? How have you seen him use that pruning to make you even more fruitful?

2. In Colossians 3:5–10, the apostle Paul lists certain things that God, the Gardener, wants to remove from our lives—all of them "dead and diseased growth." How has God pruned some of these things from your life? What things might you still struggle with that God wants to cut away?

3. What kind of fruit, or harvest, does God's discipline (pruning) develop in your life (see Hebrews 12:10–11)? How does Colossians 3:12–17 expand on this?

If we look closely at where a branch connects with a vine, it's not unusual to see sucker shoots growing around that area. The sucker shoots won't grow to bear fruit; rather, they will steal nutrients from the vine that should be going to fruit-bearing branches. The sucker shoots may seem harmless and not appear destructive, but they are distracting and steal the energy needed for the branch to bear fruit. . . . Sucker shoots require constant pruning and maintenance. The moment you prune one, it will start to grow back or a new one will pop up in its place. It's a never-ending battle.[22]

4. The moment you prune a sucker shoot, another one appears in its place. How have you seen this in your life? How do you keep sucker shoots from resprouting?

In John 15, God is described as a good gardener who is always pruning. When your way isn't working and you're connected with the vine, you have to trust the picture the pruner has in mind. When you're the one being cut, you instinctively question every clip. God is not arbitrarily cutting and snipping; he has a picture in mind. Being the branch means learning not to resist his pruning so that we can more fully experience the beautiful and fruitful life he envisions for us.[23]

5. According to Hebrews 12:6–8, when God disciplines us, it proves he loves us and we are his legitimate children. How does this help you better accept the pruning process—even when that pruning takes away something good from your life?

Pray | End your time in prayer. Ask God to make you willing for him to remove anything from your life that is hindering fruitfulness. Thank him that he loves you as his child and desires his best for you.

A PICTURE OF JESUS

If you've ever pruned a plant, you know that it can feel as if you're ruining something beautiful. But a good gardener does the hard thing because he or she has a picture in mind for the plant. Eventually, this picture becomes visible to everyone when the plant grows back stronger.

Some people think that God wants us to be happy. They think fruitfulness means getting a high-paying job or achieving a goal or maintaining physical health. Sometimes, God does give us those things. But his primary goal isn't to make us happy. His goal is to make us like Jesus.

Every plant produces what it is intended to produce. An apple tree produces apples. A pear tree produces pears. An orange tree produces oranges. A grapevine produces grapes. Likewise, if we are connected to Jesus, we will produce the fruit that we are intended to produce—"love, joy, peace, forbearance, kindness, goodness, faithfulness, gentleness and self-control" (Galatians 5:22–23).

Our natural desire is to protect ourselves from pruning. But the pruning *is* the protection. God's pruning produces deep character, perseverance, determination to overcome, humility, a new vision to serve him, love for others, a job we were actually meant for, and dependence on him for provision. If we avoid the knife, we miss this fruit.

When our way isn't working, we shouldn't avoid the pruning. Rather, we should *ask* God to prune us. It might sound strange, but here's the truth: "The pruning we ask for isn't nearly as painful as the pruning we don't ask for."[24] Embrace God's discipline and reap the harvest.

Read | John 15:1–2; Romans 8:29; Philippians 2:1–11; and 2 Timothy 2:3–7

REFLECT

1. According to John 15:2, why does the Father prune branches that are already bearing fruit? When has God pruned you in this way? How has it produced fruit?

2. In Romans 8:29, the apostle Paul says that God intended us to be "conformed to the image of his Son." Who do you know whose life reminds you of Jesus? How does that person's example inspire you to want to be more like Christ?

3. What is Jesus like, according to Philippians 2:1–11? Which of the qualities found in this passage do you most need to see developed in your own life?

4. When has God's pruning actually protected you from less-than-best and produced something new and powerful in your character or your ministry?

5. Paul wrote to Timothy, "Join with me in suffering, like a good soldier of Christ Jesus" (2 Timothy 2:3). How is this like embracing God's pruning? How do the thoughts in verses 3–7 of that passage give you courage to ask God for his pruning and trust that he will ultimately bring about a good end?

Pray | End your time in prayer. Ask God to prune you and to make you like Jesus—for your good and for God's glory.

CONNECT
& DISCUSS

Take some time today to connect with a group member and talk about some of the insights from this fourth session. Use the prompts below to guide your discussion.

How did this week's study increase your trust in God as the Gardener?

What most surprised you in this study on God's pruning? Why?

What is one thing in your life that you know God wants to prune?

What encourages you about God's purpose in disciplining you?

How can embracing God's pruning make you stronger as a believer?

How do you see God shaping you more and more into the image of Jesus?

CATCH UP &
READ AHEAD

Use this time to go back and complete any of the study and reflection questions from previous days that you weren't able to finish. Make a note below of any questions you've had, and reflect on any growth or personal insights you've gained.

Read chapters 11–12 in *When Your Way Isn't Working* before the next group session. Use the space below to make note of anything that stands out to you or encourages you from your reading.

WEEK 5

BEFORE GROUP MEETING	Read chapters 11–12 in *When Your Way Isn't Working* Read the Welcome section (page 83)
GROUP MEETING	Discuss the Connect questions Watch the video teaching for session 5 Discuss the questions that follow as a group Do the closing exercise and pray (pages 83–88)
STUDY 1	Complete the personal study (pages 90–92)
STUDY 2	Complete the personal study (pages 93–95)
STUDY 3	Complete the personal study (pages 96–97)
CONNECT & DISCUSS	Connect with someone in your group (page 98)
WRAP IT UP	Complete any unfinished personal studies (page 99) Connect with your group about the next study that you want to go through together

SESSION FIVE

GRAFTED AND GROWING

"I am the true vine."

WELCOME |

During the course of this study, we have seen how doing things our own way doesn't work. Our own way leaves us out of sorts because we are striving in our own effort. We aren't attending to our connection with Jesus.

God's way, on the other hand, is not about work at all. It's about connection first and *then* production. This is why God so carefully tends to the branches. He prunes us so we will have a healthy connection to the vine and will bear more fruit.

Now, as we come to the final session of this study, we're going to look at how easy it can be for us to loosen our hold on Jesus, the true vine, in exchange for imitation vines. Even when we know that only Jesus can produce eternal fruit in us, we attach ourselves to false vines in the hopes they will fill us up. We're especially prone to doing this when troubles come our way.

The problem with fake vines, though, is that they produce fake fruit. They never satisfy. When we let go of the true vine, the consequences are serious. We become sticks—totally fruitless and good only to be thrown into the fire!

Even then, God, in his grace, can lift us up and graft us back into the vine. But we don't have to fall away from the vine in the first place! We can hold fast to Jesus, regardless of the storms we encounter in life, and produce genuine fruit for him. This fruit will fill us with joy and will strengthen everyone around us.

CONNECT | 15 MINUTES

Get the session started by choosing one of the following questions to discuss together as a group:

- What is something that spoke to your heart in last week's personal study that you would like to share with the group?

— or —

- When things in your life get especially hard, what do you usually look to first for comfort or escape?

WATCH | 20 MINUTES

Now watch the video for this session. Below is an outline of the key points covered during the teaching. Record any key concepts that stand out to you.

OUTLINE

I. When our way isn't working, we sometimes turn from Jesus, the true vine, and pursue imitation vines.
   A. One such vine, the **information vine**, has led to information fatigue syndrome.
      1. One symptom is that more external input means less internal reflection.
      2. Another symptom is that we fail to prioritize what's important.
   B. Trying to "Google" our way out of problems has left us more confused than ever.
   C. Connecting to the information vine has left us more confused than ever.

II. Jesus is "the true vine" (John 15:1), but other imitation vines exist.
   A. The **politics vine**: we look to government to make things right in our world.
   B. The **romance vine**: we look to relationships to make things right in ourselves.
   C. The **me vine**: we look to exercise, nutrition, and self-care to make things right.
   D. If we put our hope in these things, we will be disappointed. Only connection to the **true vine** will allow us to grow and produce real fruit in our lives.

III. We can abide in Christ even when the harsh waves of life keep rolling in.
   A. Jana Robey was a follower of Christ who stayed connected to Jesus, the true vine, even when cancer robbed her of so much.
   B. She battled cancer for six-and-a-half years with incredible courage and faith.
   C. Jana's life produced much fruit because she remained in Jesus during the harshest storms of life.
   D. At the end of her life, what was Jana remembered for? Her peace, kindness, faithfulness, love, joy—the fruit of the Spirit.

IV. God can take disconnected branches and reconnect them to the vine.
   A. When we disconnect from Jesus and try to produce in our own strength, it's like expecting a dry stick to bear fruit.
   B. But the good news is that even if we *have* disconnected from Jesus, it is always possible for us to reconnect with him.
   C. God can graft us into the vine—through the blood of Jesus.
   D. No matter what storm you may face, stay connected to Jesus, the true vine.

NOTES

DISCUSS | 35 MINUTES

1. How have you witnessed the impact of "information overload"? In what ways do you think information overload has negatively affected your life and the lives of your loved ones?

2. Of the different imitation vines mentioned in the video—information, politics, romance, "me," success, wealth, entertainment, pleasure, and religion—which ones tend to most distract you from your connection with Jesus? Why do you think this is the case?

3. Which part of Jana Robey's story most impacted you? How does her love for Jesus move you to closely abide in him? How do you want the people in your life to remember you?

4. Consider this encouragement from the teaching: "The process of grafting helps us understand that connection is always possible. It's never too late to connect." How does this encourage you—regarding either your own life or the life of someone you love?

5. When have you allowed a trial in your life to draw you closer to Jesus instead of away from him? How did that impact your life going forward?

RESPOND | 10 MINUTES

Life often takes us by surprise with painful storms, and it's easy for us to seek out imitation vines to try to meet our needs. But thank the Lord, when we fall away, he can graft us back into the vine. But staying connected to Jesus, even in the hardest tests, is even better and produces beautiful fruit. Take a few minutes on your own to think about how you can draw closer to God in the midst of any storm you may be facing, and then answer the questions below.

What spoke most to your heart from the video teaching?

What is God stirring you to do as a result?

How will this strengthen your connection to Jesus?

Our connection with Jesus is the most important thing.

PRAY | 10 MINUTES

End your time by praying together as a group. As you pray, ask the Lord to reveal any imitation vines that you may be tempted to cling to and to help you abide only in him. Ask if anyone has prayer requests, and write those requests in the space below so you and your group members can continue to pray about them in the week ahead.

Name   Request

SESSION FIVE

PERSONAL STUDY

As you heard in the teaching this week, it's easy (especially when life gets hard) to try to draw life from "substitute" vines. This week you will have the chance to look at a few verses to see what the Bible says about how these imitation vines don't work and how staying connected to Jesus is the only way to produce abundant fruit. As you work through the exercises, be sure to write down your responses to the questions, as you will be given a few minutes to share your insights at the start of the next session if you are doing this study with others. If you are reading *When Your Way Isn't Working* alongside this study, first review chapters 11–12 in the book.

BEWARE OF IMITATION VINES

"Within all of us is the need to connect and the desire to produce."[25] In Jesus, we find both. Jesus, the true vine, is the answer to our longing for acceptance and purpose.

Why, then, do we so easily connect to imitation vines? We look for connection and purpose in information, politics, romance, and even religion. We get fired up about gaining a great education, or changing the world, or living happily ever after.

Some of us try the "me" vine—self-help, self-care, self-realization. But eventually, the excitement fizzles, and we end up feeling more disappointed, hurt, disillusioned, and lonely than we did before. Why is this the case?

Simply because fake vines can only produce what they are intended to produce—fake fruit. They promise the world, but true connection and purpose are found only in the fruit of a life that abides in Christ. As the evangelical Anglican bishop J.C. Ryle wrote:

> To abide in Christ means to keep up a habit of constant close communion with Him—to be always leaning on Him, resting on Him, pouring out our hearts to Him, and using Him as our Fountain of life and strength, as our chief Companion and best Friend.[26]

How beautiful is that? Why would we look to imitation vines for acceptance and purpose when Jesus is our best friend? Imitation vines will always disappoint us. Only Jesus, the true vine, gives us the acceptance and purpose we so desire.

Read | 1 Samuel 16:1-13; Colossians 3:1-4; Matthew 23:1-7; and Revelation 3:20

REFLECT

1. Think about some of the imitation vines covered in this week's group time—the information vine, the politics vine, the romance vine, and the "me" vine. Which of these vines have you been guilty of pursuing in the past? Where did pursuing those vines lead you in your life?

> When Jesus introduces the vine and the branches metaphor to the disciples in John 15, he begins by saying in verse 1, "I am the true vine." The word *true*, also translated as "real," indicates the presence of other vines that aren't true or real. Imitation vines promise to give us the nutrients we need to produce and grow, but they don't.[27]

2. Look at 1 Samuel 16:6–7. According to this passage, what does God think about fake fruit? As you review the story of David's anointing in 1 Samuel 16:1–13 as an example, how does a person who stays connected to Jesus—the *true* vine—find true connection and purpose?

3. What two things does the apostle Paul tell us to do in Colossians 3:1–4? What reason does he give? How could doing these two things help you abide in Christ and not in imitation vines?

Instead of being a branch that is connected with the true vine, I settle for being a stick with some fake fruit attached to it. From a distance nobody seems to notice. As long as I don't let anyone get too close, I get away with it. But none of it is real, and as impressive as it might look from far away, all of it is worthless. I heard an expression not long ago that I think reflects this dynamic: "Do it for the gram." Even if you've never heard this clause, you might be able to guess what it means. It's the decision to do something for the sole purpose of taking a picture and posting it on Instagram.[28]

4. Imitation vines allow us to "do it for the gram." They enable us to put up a good front and make it appear to others that we have it all together. But what did Jesus say in Matthew 23:1–7 about the Pharisees who were only concerned about keeping up their image?

5. Some people assume that Jesus' words in Revelation 3:20 are addressed to unbelievers, but Jesus is actually speaking to believers (located in the ancient city of Laodicea). In what ways might Jesus be calling you to let him draw near to you today? How will you respond to him?

Pray | End your time in prayer. Thank God that Jesus is the true vine and ask him to help you find acceptance and purpose in him alone.

RESURRECTED STICKS

We've all experienced wild storms. When the rain is pounding and the wind whipping, even an established branch can break off a tree and crash to the ground. Disconnected from its life source, the branch will eventually dry up and lose its leaves.

When our way isn't working—we lose our job, the bills pile up, someone bullies our kids, loneliness drowns us, a family member becomes ill—it's easy to let go of our hold on Jesus, the true vine. If we persist in our disconnection, we become dry and barren. We become sticks. Jesus said about sticks, "If you do not remain in me, you are like a branch that is thrown away and withers; such branches are picked up, thrown into the fire and burned" (John 15:6).

It's pretty sobering. So, is there any hope for someone who has lost connection to the vine? Well, we know that a gardener can connect a broken-off branch to a healthy tree or vine. He strips the branch clean, cuts the vine, and inserts the branch into it.

But the gardener always does the graft with a freshly cut branch that has warm sap inside it. No earthly gardener can graft a dry stick into a living tree. But God, our heavenly Gardener, "gives life to the dead and calls into being things that were not" (Romans 4:17). He can resurrect even a stick.

So when a storm knocks you down, lift up your head. Come back to Jesus and get connected to him. He wants to make you fruitful again.

Read | John 15:4-6; Mark 14:27-31; 16:6-7; Romans 4:17; and 1 Peter 5:8-11

REFLECT

1. Consider Jesus' words in John 15:4–6. What happens if you remain in the vine? What happens if you don't?

> In my office I have a stick about three feet long that sits in the corner of the room. It's a stick I found on the ground behind my house. I don't know the story of that stick. I'm not sure what kind of tree it was once connected with. My guess is that the story of this stick on the ground involves a storm. Storms have a way of turning branches into sticks.[29]

2. What storms have come your way and challenged your hold on Jesus, the true vine? How have you (or how have you not) stayed connected to him?

3. Peter, one of Jesus' disciples, fell under the pressure of a great storm. While he did not turn deliberately from God and become a dead stick, he likely feared that God was done with him after his failure. But how did Jesus show in Mark 16:7 that he still had plans for great fruitfulness in Peter? How does this encourage you?

Jesus bled so that sticks could become branches, and branches could bear good fruit. As the true vine, Jesus makes a way for sticks that have fallen off, that seem to have no purpose, and no hope to become branches once again. Jesus' death on the cross is the one thing—the only thing—that makes connection possible.[30]

4. If you have let go of your connection to Jesus, you may feel it's impossible for you to be restored. How does Jesus' death on the cross enable you to be forgiven? How does the last phrase in Romans 4:17 amplify this? Write the phrase below.

5. What are some tools that 1 Peter 5:8–11 give you to help you hold fast to Jesus in those times when storms come against you?

Pray | End your time in prayer. Thank God that he restores you when you fall and ask him to strengthen your connection to him.

HOW WILL YOU BE KNOWN?

When the family of twenty-one-year-old Jana Robey was asked to describe her, they named qualities like "joy," "peace," "kindness," "faithfulness," "love." What caused this beautiful young woman, who battled cancer for more than six years and lost so much to the disease, to radiate the fruit of the Spirit?

Jana, diagnosed at age fifteen, kept playing piano. She kept playing field hockey. When she could no longer run, she set aside her disappointment and became team manager and helped her teammates win. A second diagnosis took Jana's ability to walk, hear out of one ear, and see out of one eye. But Jana could still play piano.

For her church, she recorded a song she had written about Jesus: "You Are My Joy."[31] Jana said, "Yes, we lament in our situations, but God is with us. We can still find joy in that, in whatever we're going through."[32]

In common English, the first few fruits of the Spirit could be described like this: "The Fruit of the Spirit is an affectionate, lovable disposition, a radiant spirit and a cheerful temper, a tranquil mind and a quiet manner, a forbearing patience in provoking circumstances."[33] That's what Jana looked like.

That's what anyone connected to Jesus will look like.

How will you be known? How do you *want* to be known? If you hold onto Jesus, no matter the trial or the storm that comes your way, you will bear lasting fruit.

Read | John 10:10; 15:1–8; Galatians 5:22–23; and 2 Timothy 4:6–8

REFLECT

1. How does Jana's story impact you? When has your own difficult situation given you an opportunity to draw near to Jesus and reflect his life within you?

2. According to John 15:8, what does the Father (the Gardener) receive when we bear much fruit? What does bearing fruit show that we are?

3. Jesus explained to his followers in John 10:10 his purposes for coming to this earth. How are his words another way of talking about the fruitful life that he wants us to live?

4. In Galatians 5:22–23, Paul lists nine qualities he describes as "the fruit of the Spirit." Which of these qualities would your family members say are reflected in you? Which of these qualities do you most desire to see increased in your life?

5. When Paul penned his words in 2 Timothy 4:6–8, he knew that his death was imminent. Yet he also knew that he had lived a fruitful and abundant life in Christ. What does Paul know is in store for him next? How do these words encourage you as you conclude this study?

Pray | End your time in prayer. Thank God that he loves you so much that he allows you to share in his life, and ask him to make you fruitful as you abide in him.

CONNECT
& DISCUSS

Take some time today to connect with a group member and talk about some of the insights from this final session. Use the prompts below to guide your discussion.

What is one of the most life-changing things you learned during this study?

What are some practical things you can do to help you avoid connecting to any imitation vines?

When have you seen God resurrect someone who was a "dry stick"?

What have you learned about God's character in this study?

How can God bring you through any storm you are currently facing in a way that brings him glory?

How will you apply what you've learned in this study to deepen your connection to Jesus?

WRAP IT UP

Use this time to go back and complete any of the study and reflection questions from previous days that you weren't able to finish. Make a note below of any questions you've had and reflect on any growth or personal insights you've gained. Finally, discuss with your group what studies you might want to go through next and when you will plan on meeting together again to study God's Word.

LEADER'S

GUIDE

Thank you for your willingness to lead your group through this study! What you have chosen to do is valuable and will make a great difference in the lives of others. The rewards of being a leader are different from those of participating in a group, and we hope that as you lead, your own connection with Jesus will be deepened by this experience.

When Your Way Isn't Working is a five-session Bible study built around video content and small-group interaction. As the group leader, imagine yourself as the host of a party. Your job is to take care of your guests by managing the details so that when your guests arrive, they can focus on one another and on the interaction around the topic for that session.

Your role as the group leader is not to answer all the questions or reteach the content—the video, book, and study guide will do most of that work. Your job is to guide the experience and cultivate your small group into a connected and engaged community. This will make it a place for members to process, question, and reflect—not necessarily to receive more instruction.

There are several elements in this leader's guide that will help you as you structure your study and reflection time, so be sure to follow along and take advantage of each one.

BEFORE YOU BEGIN

Before your first meeting, make sure the group members have a copy of this study guide. Alternately, you can hand out the study guides at your first meeting and give the members some time to look over the material and ask any preliminary questions. Also, make sure they are aware that they have access to the streaming videos at any time by following the instructions printed on the study's inside front cover. During your first meeting, ask the members to provide their names, phone numbers, and e-mail addresses so that you can keep in touch with them.

Generally, the ideal size for a group is eight to ten people, which will ensure that everyone has enough time to participate in discussions. If you have more people, you might want to break up the main group into smaller subgroups. Encourage those who show up at the first meeting to commit to attending the duration of the study, as this will help the group members get to know one another, create stability for the group, and help you know how best to prepare to lead the participants through the material.

Each of the sessions in *When Your Way Isn't Working* begins with an opening reflection in the Welcome section. The questions that follow in the Connect section serve as an icebreaker to get the group members thinking about the session topic. You can go around the circle and ask each person to respond. Some people may want to tell a long story in response to one of these questions, but the goal is to keep the answers brief. Ideally, you will want everyone to get a chance to answer, so try to keep people's responses to a minute or less. If you have talkative group members, you may want to tell them up front that everyone needs to limit his or her answer to one minute.

Give the group members a chance to answer, but also tell them to feel free to pass if they wish. With the rest of the study, it's generally not a good idea to have everyone answer every question—a free-flowing discussion is more desirable. But with the opening icebreaker questions, you can go around the circle. Encourage shy people to share, but don't force them.

At your first meeting, let the group members know that each session also contains a personal study section that they can use to continue to engage with the content until the next meeting. While doing this section is optional, it will help participants cement the concepts presented during the group study time and help them better understand what it means to abide in Christ so they will bear fruit for God.

Let them know that if they choose to do so, they can watch the video for the next session by accessing the streaming code found on the inside front cover of their studies. Invite them to bring any questions and insights to your next meeting, especially if they had a breakthrough moment or didn't understand something.

PREPARATION FOR EACH SESSION

As the leader, there are a few things that you should do to best prepare for each group meeting:

- **Read through the session.** This will help you become more familiar with the content and know how to structure the discussion times.

- **Decide how the videos will be used.** Determine whether you want the members to watch the videos ahead of time (again, via the streaming access code found on the inside front cover) or together as a group.

- **Decide which questions you definitely want to discuss.** Based on the length of your group discussions, you may not be able to get through all the questions. So look over the questions listed in each session and mark which ones you definitely want to cover.

- **Be familiar with the questions you want to discuss.** When the group meets, you'll be watching the clock, so make sure you are familiar with the questions you have selected. In this way you will ensure that you have the material more deeply in your mind than your group members.

- **Pray for your group.** Pray for your group members, and ask God to lead them as they study his Word and listen to his Spirit.

Keep in mind as you lead the discussion times that in many cases there will be no one "right" answer to the questions. Answers will vary, especially when group members are being asked to share their personal experiences.

STRUCTURING THE DISCUSSION TIME

You will need to determine how long you want your group to meet each week so that you can plan your time accordingly. Suggested times for each section have been provided in this study guide, and if you adhere to these times, your group will meet for approximately ninety minutes. However, many groups like to meet for two hours. If this describes your particular group, follow the times listed in the right-hand column of the chart on the next page.

Section	90 Minutes	120 Minutes
CONNECT (discuss one or more of the opening questions for the session)	15 minutes	20 minutes
WATCH (watch the teaching material together and take notes)	20 minutes	20 minutes
DISCUSS (discuss the study questions you selected ahead of time)	35 minutes	50 minutes
RESPOND (write down key takeaways)	10 minutes	15 minutes
PRAY (pray together and dismiss)	10 minutes	15 minutes

As the group leader, it is up to you to keep track of the time and keep things on schedule. You might want to set a timer for each segment so that both you and the group members know when the time is up. (There are some good phone apps for timers that play a gentle chime or other pleasant sound instead of a disruptive noise.)

Don't be concerned if group members are quiet or slow to share. People are often quiet when they are pulling together their ideas, and this might be a new experience for some of them. Just ask a question, and let it hang in the air until someone shares. You can then say, "Thank you. What about others? What came to you when you watched that portion of the teaching?"

GROUP DYNAMICS

Leading a group through *When Your Way Isn't Working* will prove to be highly rewarding both to you and your group members. But you still may encounter challenges along the way! Discussions can get off track. Group members may not be sensitive to the needs and ideas of others. Some might worry that they will be expected to talk about matters that make them feel awkward. Others may express comments that result in disagreements. To help ease this strain on you and the group, consider the following ground rules:

- When someone raises a question or comment that is off the main topic, suggest that you deal with it another time, or, if you feel led in that direction, let the group know that you will be spending some time discussing it.

- If someone asks a question that you don't know how to answer, admit it, and move on. At your discretion, feel free to invite group members to comment on questions that call for personal experience.

- If you find that one or two people are dominating the discussion time, direct a few questions to others in the group. Outside the main group time, ask the more dominating members to help you draw out the quieter ones. Work to make them part of the solution instead of part of the problem.

- When a disagreement occurs, encourage the group members to process the matter in love. Encourage those on opposite sides to restate what they heard the other side say about the matter, and then invite each side to evaluate if that perception is accurate. Lead the group in examining other passages of Scripture related to the topic, and look for common ground.

When any of these issues arise, encourage your group members to follow these words from Scripture: "Love one another" (John 13:34); "If it is possible, as far as it depends on you, live at peace with everyone" (Romans 12:18); "Whatever is true, . . . noble, . . . right, . . . if anything is excellent or praiseworthy—think about such things" (Philippians 4:8); and, "Be quick to listen, slow to speak and slow to become angry" (James 1:19). This will make your group time more rewarding and beneficial for everyone who attends.

Thank you again for taking the time to lead your group. You are making a difference in your group members' lives and having an impact on their journey toward a better understanding of how staying connected to Jesus will not only bring about the fruitful life that he desires for each of us but will also bring God glory.

ABOUT THE AUTHOR

Kyle Idleman is the senior pastor at Southeast Christian Church in Louisville, Kentucky, one of the largest churches in America. On a normal weekend, he speaks to more than twenty-five thousand people spread across many campuses. More than anything else, Kyle enjoys unearthing the teachings of Jesus and making them relevant in people's lives. He is a frequent speaker for national conventions and influential churches across the country. Kyle and his wife, DesiRae, have been married for over twenty-five years. They have four children, two sons-in-law, and recently welcomed their first grandchild. They live on a farm in Kentucky, where he does no farming.

ENDNOTES

1. Kyle Idleman, *When Your Way Isn't Working* (Grand Rapids, MI: Zondervan, 2023), 4.

2. Idleman, *When Your Way Isn't Working*, 7–8.

3. Idleman, *When Your Way Isn't Working*, 4–6.

4. Idleman, *When Your Way Isn't Working*, 9–10.

5. Idleman, *When Your Way Isn't Working*, 32.

6. Idleman, *When Your Way Isn't Working*, 29.

7. Idleman, *When Your Way Isn't Working*, 36.

8. Idleman, *When Your Way Isn't Working*, 45.

9. Idleman, *When Your Way Isn't Working*, 47.

10. Samuel Chadwick (1860–1932), *The Way to Pentecost* (Fort Washington, PA: CLC, 2000), 116–117.

11. Chadwick, *The Way to Pentecost*, 108.

12. Idleman, *When Your Way Isn't Working*, 109–110.

13. Idleman, *When Your Way Isn't Working*, 118.

14. Kyle teaches more fully on the topic of connection with other people in chapter 10, "Tangled Up," in *When Your Way Isn't Working*.

15. These thoughts about being with Jesus are laid out in Jim Cymbala, "More Than a Relationship (Fellowship with God)," video, The Believer: Simple Truths about Following Jesus, accessed February 22, 2023, https://www.brooklyntabernacle.org/grow-2/the-believer/more-than-a-relationship/.

16. Idleman, *When Your Way Isn't Working*, 115–116.

17. Idleman, *When Your Way Isn't Working*, 119.

18. Translators decide which meaning to give a word based on the context of the passage in which it is found. Most translators lean toward "cuts off" for the Greek word *airo* in John 15:2 rather than "picks up," the other meaning for the word, possibly because John 15:6 talks about branches that do *not* remain in Christ and are then thrown away and burned. But in John 15:2, the branch *does* remain in Christ—but for some reason doesn't bear fruit. Since Jesus said in John 15:5 that every branch that remains in him would bear fruit, the context here could easily lend itself to "picks up" so that the fruitless branch could become healthy again and begin bearing fruit, as it should.

19. Kyle digs more deeply into the topic of how we as believers need each other in chapter 10, "Tangled Up," in *When Your Way Isn't Working*.

20. Idleman, *When Your Way Isn't Working*, 134–135.

21. Idleman, *When Your Way Isn't Working*, 136.

22. Idleman, *When Your Way Isn't Working*, 150–151.

23. Idleman, *When Your Way Isn't Working*, 142–143.

24. Idleman, *When Your Way Isn't Working*, 154.

25. Idleman, *When Your Way Isn't Working*, 195.

26. J.C. Ryle (1816–1900), *Ryle's Expository Thoughts on the Gospels*, John 15, verses 7–11, Studylight.org, accessed February 15, 2023, https://www.studylight.org/commentaries/eng/ryl/john-15.html.

27. Idleman, *When Your Way Isn't Working*, 196.
28. Idleman, *When Your Way Isn't Working*, 199.
29. Idleman, *When Your Way Isn't Working*, 198–199. Kyle focuses in on the topic of how storms can grow us and connect us more deeply to Christ in chapter 11, "Growing Pains," in *When Your Way Isn't Working*.
30. Idleman, *When Your Way Isn't Working*, 206–7.
31. Interview of Jana Robey by Kyle Idleman, "I Call to Mind," podcast, One at a Time, accessed February 21, 2023, https://podcasts.apple.com/us/podcast/i-call-to-mind/id1451611909?i=1000457896240.
32. "Louisville Woman Whose Music Inspired Many Dies of Brain Cancer," WDRB.com, August 20, 2020, https://www.wdrb.com/news/louisville-woman-whose-music-inspired-many-dies-of-brain-cancer/article_63e4522a-e32f-11ea-84d0-ff63af8a96be.html.
33. Chadwick, *The Way to Pentecost*, 138–139.

Also Available from
KYLE IDLEMAN

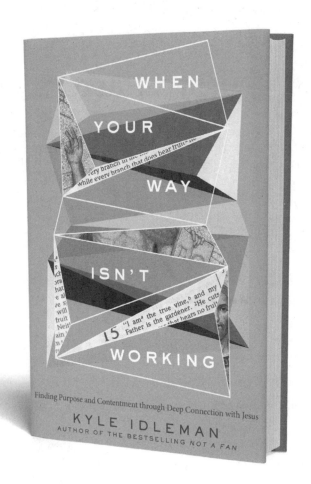

4◉ DAYS THROUGH THE BOOK

Study Books of the Bible with Trusted Pastors

The 40 Days Through the Book series has been designed to help believers more actively engage with God's Word. Each study encourages participants to read through one book in the New Testament at least once during the course of 40 days and provides them with:

- A clear understanding of the background and culture in which the book was written,

- Insights into key passages of Scripture, and

- Clear applications and takeaways from the particular book that participants can apply to their lives.

Available now at your favorite bookstore, or streaming video on StudyGateway.com.

HarperChristian Resources

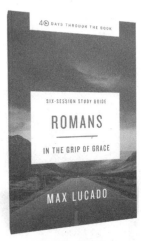

ROMANS
In The Grip Of Grace

Max Lucado

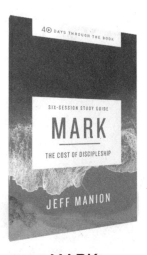

MARK
The Cost Of Discipleship

Jeff Manion

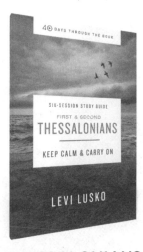

THESSALONIANS
Keep Calm & Carry On

Levi Lusko

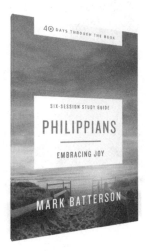

PHILIPPIANS
Embracing Joy

Mark Batterson

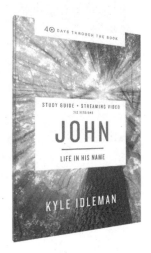

JOHN
Life in His Name

Kyle Idleman

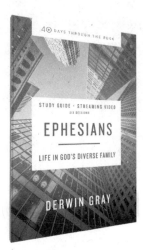

EPHESIANS
Life in God's Diverse Family

Derwin Gray

HarperChristian Resources

ALSO AVAILABLE

Bible Study Guide + Streaming Video   DVD

Available now at your favorite bookstore
or streaming video on StudyGateway.com.

The Jesus Bible Study Series

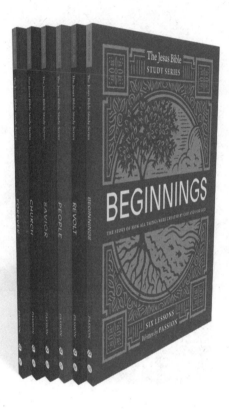

Beginnings
ISBN 9780310154983

Revolt
ISBN 9780310155003

People
ISBN 9780310155027

Savior
ISBN 9780310155041

Church
ISBN 9780310155065

Forever
ISBN 9780310155089

Available wherever books are sold

 passionpublishing    Harper*Christian* Resources

From the Publisher

GREAT STUDIES

ARE EVEN BETTER WHEN THEY'RE SHARED!

Help others find this study:

- Post a review at your favorite online bookseller.

- Post a picture on a social media account and share why you enjoyed it.

- Send a note to a friend who would also love it—or, better yet, go through it with them!

Thanks for helping others grow their faith!

Accept Him

Get connected   John 15:5

Know Him   John 17:3

Make Him everything Phil

Tommy